PLAY BY PLAY

MOUNTAIN BIKING

The following athletes were
photographed for this book:
Lauren Flagg,
Talisyn Flagg,
Brian Fuller,
Jerad Fuller,
Jason Garza,
Ryan Gaul,
Jake Harper,
Nicole Hektner,
Kevin Ivy,
Josh Otzen,
Mike Tucker.

LERNER
SPORTS
AN IMPRINT OF LERNER PUBLISHING GROUP

PLAY BY PLAY

MOUNTAIN BIKING

Text and photographs by Andy King

Lerner Publications Company ● Minneapolis

To Pat and Molly

LernerSports
An imprint of Lerner Publishing Group
241 First Avenue North
Minneapolis, MN 55401 U.S.A.

Website address: www.lernerbooks.com

Library of Congress Cataloging-in-Publication Data

King, Andy.
    Play-by-play mountain biking / text and photographs by Andy King. -- Rev. ed.
        p.   cm.—(Fundamental sports)
    Rev. ed. of: Fundamental mountain biking. c1997.
    Includes bibliographical references (p.) and index.
    Summary: An introduction to the sport of mountain biking, including an explanation of the required equipment and necessary skills.
        ISBN 0-8225-9879-5 (pbk. : alk. paper)
    1. All terrain cycling—Juvenile literature. [1. All terrain cycling.] I. King, Andy. Fundamental mountain biking. II. Title.
    GV1056 .K54   1997
    796.6'3—dc21   00-008852

Manufactured in the United States of America
1 2 3 4 5 6 – GPS – 06 05 04 03 02 01

Photo Acknowledgments
Photos reproduced with permission of: pp. 8, 10 (both), © Wende Cragg; p. 9, Haynes Foundation Collection, Montana Historical Society; p. 33, Courtesy GT Bicycles; p. 35 (top left), © Nathan Bilow, Courtesy Fat Tire Bike Week; p. 35 (top right), © Xani Fané, Courtesy Fat Tire Bike Week; pp. 42, 62, Courtesy Cannondale Corporation.

Diagram on pp. 14–15 courtesy of *All Action Mountain Biking,* by Bob Allen, published by Wayland Publishers Limited. All other diagrams and artwork by Laura Westlund.

CONTENTS

Chapter 1

HOW THIS SPORT GOT STARTED

Do you ever wish you could fly through a forest like an owl? Or follow a trail like a deer, leaves crackling beneath you? Have you ever wanted to whiz through the trees as the sun streamed through the leaves?

One sport combines the fast pace of bike riding with the enjoyment of seeing nature up close. That sport is mountain biking. On a bike, you can climb hills and jump logs in your path. You can test your sense of balance and your reflexes on challenging courses. You can follow a path or make your own.

"Repack" is the name of a hill in Marin County, California. In the 1970s, mountain bike racing first became popular on this hill, which drops 1,300 feet in less than 2 miles. Riders had to repack, or replace the grease that sizzled out of the coaster brakes after lunging down this steep hill. Coaster brakes are brakes that stop a bike when the rider pedals backward. The hill became known as "Repack" to those who rode it. The last Repack race was run in 1984.

BEGINNINGS OF BIKING

The first bicycles were created in the early 1800s. These bicycles didn't look much like the bikes we have. Early bicycles were awkward and difficult to control. Still, people enjoyed the freedom that bicycles gave them. As mechanics kept improving the design, more people bought bicycles. By about 1890, bicycles with inflatable tires and adjustable handlebars were available.

Off-road bikes had a very practical beginning about this time. Military leaders thought bikes would be a way to quickly transport soldiers around battlefields. In the late 1890s, the U.S. Army formed the Twenty-fifth Bicycle Corps Regiment. These soldiers rode bikes that weighed 90 pounds. The bikes were made of sturdy metal to handle harsh conditions.

In June 1897, Corps members rode their bikes 1,900 miles from their base camp in Missoula, Montana, to St. Louis, Missouri, to test the combat readiness of the bikes. Although the bikes passed this difficult test, the U. S. Army rarely used bikes. Instead, the military's engineers developed motorized methods of transportation.

In the 1950s, a bicycle enthusiast named John Finley Scott began altering bicycles so he could ride them

Members of the Twenty-fifth Bicycle Corps of the U.S. Army climb a hill in Montana in 1896.

off-road. On mountain trails in Oregon and California, Scott rode a bicycle with **balloon tires** and **gears**.

Scott's bikes didn't catch on in the '50s, but later, in the 1970s, other bicyclists wanted to go down the rolling hills in northern California at top speeds. Gary Fisher, Charlie Kelly, Joe Breeze, Tom Ritchey, and Wende Cragg were just some of the cyclists who loved to race down the hills in Marin County, California. They rode modified **beach-cruising bikes,** or clunkers, as they called them. They put together parts from many types of bikes to make their clunkers.

Above, Joe Breeze, left, and Charlie Kelly were some of the first bicyclists to take their bikes off the regular paths. Below, Kelly heads down Repack Hill.

The Californians used **fat tires** with deep treads for good **traction** on the steep dirt hills. Their early bikes had problems, however. Some hills were too steep to ride, which meant the riders had to push their bikes up the hill. Going downhill wasn't without problems, either. The bikes' **brakes** were made of metal and lubricated with grease. When a rider who was going fast tried to stop, friction in the brakes melted the grease. The grease ran out of the brake. After each run down a hill, the rider would have to repair the bike by replacing, or repacking, grease into the brakes.

Fisher, Kelly, and the others kept making improvements to their bikes. They made an extra-tough **frame** so that a bike would last longer despite the rough rides. They developed better brake and gear systems. They flattened the bike's handlebars for better control. The mountain bike was born. By 1981, companies were making mountain bikes after the pattern of the old clunkers. In 1996, 20 years after off-road racing began, mountain biking made its debut in the Summer Olympic Games. Modern mountain bikes are made of strong, lightweight metals such as aluminum, steel, and titanium. These bikes often weigh less than 25 pounds.

A modern mountain bike has a suspension system, or set of springs, for absorbing the shocks that bikers encounter. A mountain bike has from 15 to 21 speeds to help a rider handle any hill.

Chapter 2

BASICS

Although most bicycles can be ridden off-road, many street bikes can be damaged by off-road conditions. It's a good idea to have a mountain bike for use on rough off-road surfaces.

All mountain bikes have several basic parts. First, a mountain bike has a strong frame so that the bumps and jolts of the road, and the occasional spills, won't damage it.

A mountain bike also has tires that are wider than regular street bike tires. These tires are called fat tires or knobbies. A knobby gets its name from the raised rubber bumps of its deep tread. The wide, deep tread gives the bike better traction on rough paths and helps to absorb the bumps. These fat tires also make the bike more stable and are less likely to puncture, even on rough roads.

Mountain bike gears are different from street bike gears. A mountain bike has 15 to 21 gears instead of the 10 or fewer gears other bikes have. Extra gears enable riders to pedal up hills and on flats with ease.

Mountain bike tires have deep, knobby treads. The tires come in various colors with different tread patterns.

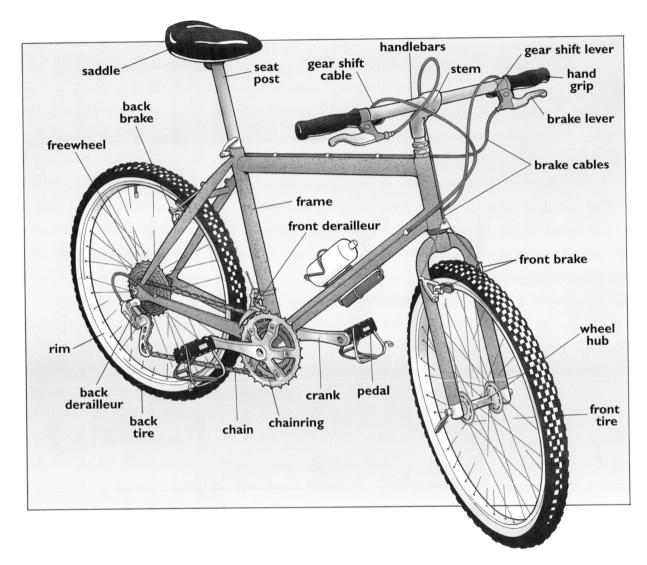

saddle
seat post
back brake
freewheel
gear shift cable
handlebars
stem
gear shift lever
hand grip
brake lever
brake cables
frame
front derailleur
front brake
rim
wheel hub
back derailleur
back tire
chain
chainring
crank
pedal
front tire

A bike's chain follows the teeth of the chainring, which is connected to the pedal **cranks.** The chain goes around a freewheel on the back tire hub. When you pedal, the chainring turns, turning the chain. The chain moves the freewheel, which turns the rear wheel. The chainring and freewheel have sprockets, or toothed wheels, of different sizes.

The gear shift lever on the right side of the handlebars operates the back **derailleur** (dih-RAY-luhr), or gear-switching operation. The gear shift lever on the left controls the front derailleur on the large chainring.

By moving the chain to different sprockets, you can change the gear you are in. This helps you to maintain a steady speed. Pedaling will become easier or more difficult, depending on the gear you choose. The number of sprockets your bike has will determine how many gears it has. For example, if your bike has three front sprockets and six rear sprockets, it has 18 gears.

When the bike is in a high gear, the chain is on a large sprocket in front and a small freewheel track. This chain position helps the rider go fast on flat ground. In a high gear, one turn of the pedals turns the rear wheel about three times. That moves the bike about 21 feet. High gears are for speed!

When a rider needs power—to climb a hill, for example—the rider switches into a lower gear by shifting the chain to a smaller sprocket on the front and a larger sprocket on the back tire's freewheel. In a low gear, one turn of the pedal turns the rear wheel only once and the bike moves about 7 feet.

The brake levers are also located on the handlebars. The back brake lever is on the right side, and the front

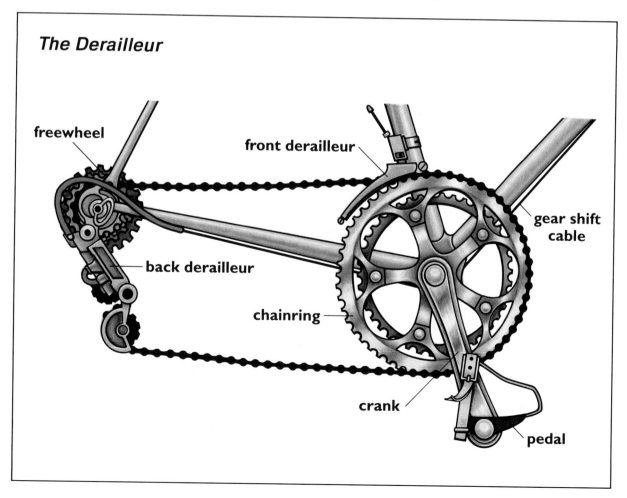

The Derailleur

freewheel

front derailleur

gear shift cable

back derailleur

chainring

crank

pedal

As the riders above show, bike gloves and helmets come in all sorts of styles and colors.

Bike shop owners can straighten, or "true," a wheel for you if one is bent out of shape.

brake lever is on the left. Because off-road terrain varies greatly, a rider needs good brakes to quickly control the bike's speed.

Brakes stop the bike by keeping the wheels from turning. When you squeeze a brake lever, two pads—one on each side of the wheel—clamp against it. The brake pads will slow the wheel if you squeeze lightly on the levers. The wheel stops if you squeeze the levers tightly.

The way a bicycle fits a rider is very important. Off-road bikes shouldn't be too small or too large. Here's one way to get a good fit. Standing over the bicycle's bar, you should have about 2 to 4 inches of room between your crotch and the bike.

Find a comfortable sitting position that allows you to reach the gear-shifting lever and the brake lever on each side. The seat of a mountain bike is set farther back than the seat of a street bike. Adjust the **saddle,** or seat, and the handlebars so that your feet rest on the pedals with your knees slightly bent. Try to find a bike that is equipped with **toeclips.** The clips hold your feet securely, but they also release easily if you need to put your feet on the ground.

Mountain bikes cost from $200 for a basic bike to thousands of dollars for a racing bike. It's always a good idea to make sure your bike is in good condition. An overhaul every once in a while will help ensure that your bike won't break down. A bicycle repair shop can help you keep your bike in good condition. Most bikes require special tools for maintenance on the cranks, **wheel hubs,** and **spokes.**

Before you try any off-road bicycling, get the right equipment. It's a good idea to wear a helmet whenever you ride a bike, but it's most important to have one when you're riding off-road. You are sure to meet unexpected obstacles, and your chances of crashing are much greater when you're off-road. Helmets are made of foam and hard plastic. Be sure you get a helmet that meets safety standards and replace it if it gets cracked.

PEDALS

Bike pedals are your point of contact with your bike. This contact drives the bike. Two items of equipment—toeclips and clipless pedals with matching shoes—help ensure a good connection between the pedals and your feet. These devices allow you to pull up the pedals with the pedaling motion as well as push them down.

Toeclips, as shown above, hold your feet on the pedals with a cage around your toes. It's easy to pull out of them if necessary, and toeclips don't require special shoes. Clipless pedals with matching shoes, as shown below, have latches on the pedals and the shoes. They are attached and detached by a twist of the foot.

TRAIL SAFETY

Some rules of the trail will help you have a successful and fun ride. The following are from the International Mountain Bicycling Association:

1. Only ride on open trails on which bikes are allowed.
2. Leave no trace. Don't cause extra erosion on dirt trails by **skidding.** And never litter.
3. Ride under control to protect yourself and others on the trails.
4. Be considerate of hikers and other bikers. Slow down or stop when approaching others. A friendly greeting or bell can signal your approach.
5. When encountering animals, slow down and pass at a safe distance.
6. Think ahead. Make sure you have the right equipment and training.
7. Wear a helmet and pay attention to the weather.

Glasses or goggles will help protect your eyes from branches. Padded gloves help absorb shocks and make gripping the handlebars easier. Bike shoes have rigid soles to provide even pressure on your feet while pedaling. Even pressure makes pushing the pedals more comfortable, and you'll have more power as you turn your pedals. Biking shorts have padding that will help to prevent soreness from your saddle. Biking jerseys are cool and comfortable.

One of the best things about a mountain bike is that you can ride it on nearly any terrain. Finding a good location to ride a mountain bike will take some exploring. Many local and state parks open their trails to bikers. In some states, ski areas allow mountain bikers to ride on the slopes during the off-season.

Ride carefully on a new or unfamiliar trail, and of course, don't ride if the trail is marked as private property. Hikers or horseback riders may share your trails. If you meet someone on the trail, be courteous and allow others the right-of-way.

Let's follow Josh and Ryan on their mountain bike ride to see where they go. They start their ride at Josh's house, where they check their tires' **air pressure** and look over their bikes for mechanical problems. Then Josh and Ryan put on their helmets and leave the garage.

Riding through their neighborhood, they pay attention to the traffic and obey the traffic signs. After a short ride, they reach a park trail where they will begin their adventure.

As soon as Ryan and Josh go off-road, they feel the difference in the terrain. The dirt path is not smooth like the street. Josh takes a more comfortable position on his bike.

Always looking ahead, Ryan and Josh keep their arms slightly bent and their legs pedaling. They go down a small hill with rocks at the bottom. Josh and Ryan ride over the small rocks and around the big ones.

Pedaling fast to pick up speed, Ryan and Josh start up a hill. When Ryan feels his pedaling pace slow, he shifts gears to make pedaling easier. Josh shifts down, too. The two work hard to make it to the top. As they reach the crest of the hill, their hearts are pounding rapidly.

Then the fun starts all over again. Josh and Ryan head down the path, picking up speed as they go.

FIXING A FLAT

Riding off-road is hard on bikes, so some repair work is inevitable. One of the most common problems is a flat tire. Fortunately, you can be back on your bike in minutes once you know how to fix a flat. You will need prying bars for taking the tire off, a tube patch kit, and a pump (pictured above). Bike stores sell pry tools and tire patch kits.

To change a tire, first open the tire valve. The valve is attached to your tire and sticks up through the rim. Release any remaining air out of the valve by pressing down the valve stem.

Slide your prying tools down between the rim and the tire on either side of the valve. Pry the tire back and up over the edge of the rim. Once you have the tire over the rim, continue to pull one side of the tire out over the rim. Then push the valve out through the hole in the rim. Look for the cause of the flat on the inside and outside of the tire. Next, find the leak on the tube. You may have to pump air into the tire to find the leak. Once you've inflated the tire, listen for air leaking or lightly touch the tire to feel any air escaping. If the leak is slow or very hard to find, dunk the tire in water and look for bubbles. Once you find the leak, mark the spot and deflate the tire.

Clean the surface of the tire as best you can. Then scrape it with the roughing tool in the kit. Be sure to mark where the leak is because sometimes it will be hard to spot after this step. Apply the adhesive to an area larger than the patch you selected. Most adhesives must dry slightly, until tacky, before you can apply the patch. Remove the backing from the patch and apply it to the area. Press evenly on the patch and hold for a minute or more.

Put the tube back on the rim inside the tire, starting with the valve through the rim. Insert the tube around the whole tire and pull the tire over the rim. Once the tire is on the wheel, pump it up about a third full. Push the side of the tire to make sure the tube is not twisted or off-center in the tire. Then inflate the tire to the correct pressure for your tires. (The suggested pressure per square inch, p.s.i, will be on the side of the tire.) Put your wheel back on your bike and enjoy the rest of your ride!

Chapter 3

MANEUVERS

A mountain bike gives a rider the freedom to go almost anywhere because the bike can handle almost any terrain. You probably already know how to ride a bicycle. Before venturing off-road though, be sure you can control your bike.

Mountain biking makes use of all your cycling skills. The demanding terrain and frequent obstacles require an off-road cyclist to have good balance and complete control of his or her mountain bike.

Talisyn, at right, knows that pedaling fast will help her maintain her balance. As her forward motion increases, she is less likely to tip.

When starting out, Talisyn shifts her weight slightly and turns the handlebars to balance herself. Once she has gained speed, her balance will be controlled mainly by her forward **momentum.**

Some turns are "natural" and others are "forced." Natural turns are made over long distances, allowing the rider and bike to flow smoothly in a different direction. Forced turns are quicker and require more action from the cyclist.

Lauren is making a natural turn. She gradually leans through the long

bend in the trail. Notice that she doesn't move her handlebars much. The turn is controlled mostly by her slight lean.

As Lauren begins to make a left-hand turn, she leans left, into the turn. By doing this, she changes the position of her bike. If Lauren didn't lean, the force of the turn would send her body away from the direction she wants to go. That push could make her crash.

As Lauren feels the bike shift, she turns the handlebars to the left to complete the turn. Then, she moves the handlebars back to the center position and shifts her weight so it's balanced over the bike. When Lauren turns to the right, she leans right. The more you ride, the more comfortable you will feel while turning and balancing.

It's important to know how your bike will respond to your actions. No turn is the same as another. Lauren is moving slowly, so she doesn't lean much to complete her turn. Just a slight shift of her weight and a slight turn of the handlebars allows her to change direction. As Lauren's speed increases, her lean must also increase. When she goes through a fast turn, she must lean more dramatically to counter the forces of gravity that pull her away from the direction of the turn.

A log in Lauren's path requires her to make a forced turn. She doesn't lean much in the turn, but she turns her handlebars quickly to make it around the log. Lauren is ready to handle any turns on the path.

BRAKING

Brakes control your speed as well as stop your bike. Brakes should be adjusted to allow you to slow your wheels with a light squeeze and stop them with a firmer one. Your right hand controls the rear brakes, and your left hand operates the front brakes. To brake smoothly, squeeze both brakes with even pressure.

Braking is done in different ways, according to the situation. Kevin demonstrates how to use a mountain bike's brakes.

The front brakes are stronger than the back brakes. If Kevin brakes only with his front brakes, his front tire will slow down more than the rear tire. Kevin's momentum will push him forward, over the handlebars. He might crash and do an uncomfortable maneuver known as a "faceplant."

If Kevin squeezes only the rear brakes, the rear tire will slow down more than the front tire. If that happens, the rear tire might **fishtail,** or swing from side to side.

Riding downhill requires special techniques. As Kevin descends, he stays low and keeps his weight back, nearly over his back wheel. Gravity is pulling his body forward and down the hill, so it's important for Kevin to stay off and behind his saddle. He is careful to not apply too much pressure to his front brake.

Mike, below, can better control his bike when his tires are rolling than when they are sliding, so he lightly squeezes his brakes and releases them. This is called **feathering.** With practice, Mike can control his speed down even the toughest hills.

Skidding to a halt is fun but damages the trail. To keep trails in good shape, keep skids to a minimum.

The shifter in the photo above is a grip shifter. To shift gears with this type of shifter, you turn the knob to the number of the gear you want to use. The brake lever is in front of the handlebar. The shifter in the photo below is a thumb shifter. To shift gears with this type of shifter, you move the small lever with your thumb. The brake lever is again in front of the handlebars.

PEDALING AND GEARS

By pedaling, your legs provide the power to "run" your bike. Gears maximize your power. Low gears allow you to turn the pedals rapidly, making uphill riding easier. The high gears are for going fast.

A rider needs coordination to shift gears. As you approach a hill, shift from a high gear to a low gear. Before you lose your speed from the flat section, use your left shifter to move the front chainring to a smaller sprocket. Still pedaling, use your right hand to shift the freewheel to a larger sprocket, or track. The hill will begin to slow your progress, but you can speed up your pedaling.

Shifting gears takes practice. As you ride your mountain bike, you'll learn to use all the levels of the gearing system. You'll keep your momentum if you **spin,** or pedal continuously.

Shifting gears keeps your pedals turning at an even rate. In too high a gear, you may have to push too hard. In too low a gear, you'll turn your pedals too fast for the speed you are going.

Once you become an accomplished mountain biker, you will achieve a flow. Putting steering, braking, and shifting into this flow requires skill that you will develop with practice. Instead of thinking about shifting or turning, you will do it naturally. Most riders make their bikes an extension of themselves. When you run, you think about running faster and your legs start moving faster. It's the same with mountain biking. The best riders are experts at combining maneuvers so that they react to the road.

Chapter 4

COMPETITION

One way to test your mountain biking ability is to compete in off-road races. Off-road races are held in downhill, cross-country, uphill, and observed trials. Competition comes from other racers, the clock, and the challenging courses you will face.

The National Off-Road Bicycle Association (NORBA) is the part of the United States Cycling Federation that organizes national and local off-road races. NORBA began in 1983. It maintains rules and standards for races.

World championships are held in the United States and Europe. More races are being held around the country every year. You can find out about races from newspapers or bike shops in your area.

RACES

Downhill racers follow a course, which usually starts at the top of a hill. They travel down through a series of gates that are marked by flags or plastic poles. Some races are time trials, which means the cyclists are timed as they go down the course, one by one. If the gates are close together, the downhill race is called a

OFF-ROAD CHAMPION

Juli Furtado was on the U. S. National Ski Team before knee injuries forced her to explore other sports. She began bicycle road racing and in 1989 became a professional mountain bike racer. During her career, Juli was a two-time World Champion and a five-time National Champion. She raced in the 1996 Olympics before contracting the disease called lupus. She retired in 1997.

slalom race. Slalom races pit two racers against each other on side-by-side courses. Nerves of steel, as well as a sturdy bike, are needed for this race. High speeds mean a high number of crashes.

Cross-country races require racers to follow a course. Courses can be in the shape of a circle, or they can go from one location to another. A cross-country race is often the featured event during mountain biking festivals. Cross-country races can vary from 10 to 100 miles. Cross-country races are shorter for beginning riders than for advanced and professional riders.

Uphill courses test a racer's ability to climb hills. This event calls for strength and endurance. Uphill events may be slow. The winner is the cyclist who reaches the top of the hill in the shortest amount of time.

In competitions called observed trials, skill, not speed, is the key. The bikes used in this event are small and are geared lower to give cyclists more control. Riders must maneuver over and around a course full of obstacles such as rocks and logs. The riders try to finish the course without putting a foot on the ground. They are penalized if they touch the ground and if they don't complete an obstacle.

MORE WAYS TO RIDE

Off-road bikes are a great form of transportation. Here are some other uses for a mountain bike:

Bicycle polo, above: Instead of riding horses, bicycle polo players ride bikes. On a grass field, riders try to hit a ball with mallets through the other team's goal.

Bicycle limbo, above right: Riding a bike under a pole that is lowered, little by little, is called bicycle limbo. Limbo is one of the most popular events at the annual Fat Tire Bike Week in Colorado.

Bike cops at right: Most large city police forces have officers that regularly patrol on mountain bikes.

Mountain bike tours: A mountain bike vacation is a great way to see the country from the saddle of your bike. Colorado and California are popular destinations.

COMPETITION

Let's follow Jason as he competes in a cross-country race. After several months of training, Jason decided to ride in his first race. It's a two-lap race, so he will ride nearly five miles.

Arriving before the race, Jason registers, pays the entry fee, and gets a number. He puts that number on the front of his bike. The racers will start the race in groups, or heats. The race starter calls the riders to the line by number. Soon it's time for Jason's group to take the course.

As the pack of riders thins out, Jason picks up speed for the first **straightaway.** The course goes into the trees. Jason relies on his technical skills to make the tight turns and jump the tree roots on the path.

Emerging from the trees, Jason sees a short downhill stretch that leads to another hill. He must pedal hard to climb the hill, and he feels sweat running down his neck.

As Jason rides, he feels his heart pounding, and he struggles to keep his legs pumping the pedals. He rounds a corner, and a few spectators

cheer encouragement. The course turns and heads up a steep, rocky hill. Jason stays low and leans back on his bike, legs pumping.

Jason absorbs the bumps going over rocks on the track. Jason's hours of riding with friends are paying off as he heads into the last lap. He feels good. Riding faster than the first lap, Jason zooms through the trees.

He starts up the last big hill before the finish line. His legs start to feel like rubber, but he cranks up the hill. When he's nearly to the top, he slows down too much. His bike stalls and he has to jump off and push it up the last few feet. Then he jumps back on his bike. Breathing hard after the hill, Jason looks ahead to the finish line. He wants to finish the race strong so he pushes hard. Jason finishes in fourth place in his age category. His mom and brother congratulate him as he takes a long drink of water.

You might not always finish a race first, but there are personal victories in competition, too. Making it to the top of a steep hill could be a victory. So can going faster than your previous best time. These personal victories, and the fun of riding with others, make off-road racing a great way to have fun.

PRACTICE, PRACTICE

Chapter 5

Mountain bike practice means riding. To be a good cyclist, a person needs endurance, strength, and technical skills. Kevin, Jerad, Brian, and Lauren will show us how they practice these skills to become better riders.

To train for a race, they first set up a riding schedule for themselves. One day they will train for endurance. The next day they will combine strength training with technical skills training. Before every ride, they stretch slowly.

ENDURANCE TRAINING

On the first day, Jerad and Brian work on their endurance. Their goal is to be able to ride for an hour or more without becoming tired and out of breath.

The best way to train for endurance is to take long rides on paved roads. At the beginning, a long ride might be a 45-minute ride without stops. Riders can continue for longer periods as their endurance grows.

To build their endurance, they want to keep their heart rates at a

consistently high level. They ride on roads to maintain a constant and steady pedaling, or spinning, pace. Off-road riding is more fun, but it requires quick bursts of energy rather than the sustained rate needed for building endurance.

Jerad and Brian ride around a park. They set a pace that they can maintain for a long time. They ride so they won't be out of breath, but their breathing is noticeable. They will ride like this for an hour.

The next day, they decide to do strength training. Kevin knows of a steep hill that they can climb to build their power.

STRENGTH TRAINING

After stretching and warming up by riding around for several minutes, Kevin is ready to train. As he starts to climb, he practices shifting gears and staying in his seat. He keeps his pedals spinning as he cranks to the top of the hill. Once at the top, he turns around and goes down. Slowing down at the bottom, he turns around and rides up again.

Training on hills is difficult. It's important to start slowly. Try the hill two or three times. Later, as your strength and endurance increase, you can increase the number of times you go up the hill.

FROM BMX TO MOUNTAINS

Growing up in Los Angeles, Tinker Juarez developed outstanding off-road bike skills by riding in bicycle motocross (BMX) competitions near his home. Following a successful BMX career, Tinker became a professional mountain bike racer when he was 28 years old.

Tinker developed his endurance and became one of the top mountain bike racers in the world. He won a gold medal at the 1995 Pan American Games, and he was the first American to finish at the 1996 Olympics, placing 19th overall. He struggled through the 1997 season but returned to his winning form in 1998.

Kevin knows that using low gears makes climbing the hill easier. Using a low gear causes the rear tire to spin faster. But to have a good grip, or traction, the tire needs weight on it. When Kevin stays on his seat, his weight is over the rear tire. As he goes up the hill, he changes gears.

He might not be able to climb the hill by staying in his seat. To push himself to the top, Kevin stands on his pedals to increase his power. He keeps his weight back so that the rear tire doesn't lose traction. He pulls up on the front of the bike.

BIKE-HANDLING SKILLS

Bike-handling skills are another part of off-road training. During rides, try to find a difficult path with trees and many tight turns. Maybe you can even find a path with a log or two.

Lauren shows how she handles a short stretch she found. She winds through the start of the path. A depression in the trail forces her to stand. She absorbs the impact as her front tire drops quickly and then jumps up. Lauren then shifts to a low gear to push up the short hill. Picking up speed, she leans around two trees and ducks under a branch.

Seeing a log in her path, she pulls on her handlebars to raise her front tire in the air. As her front tire starts over the log, Lauren shifts her weight forward to allow the rear of her bike to roll over the log.

One of the great things about mountain biking is that every time you ride, you gain experience. This experience will help you find your own way of training. Sometimes, you may want to try ending a long ride with a few repetitions on some hills. Or you may decide to try working on technical skills throughout a long ride. The more you ride on any surface, the more your skills will improve.

Chapter 6

RAZZLE DAZZLE

Observed trials riders are some of the most highly skilled bike riders around. Many can **hop** up and over logs or large rocks. Even if you don't specialize in observed trials, you can learn how to control your bike at all times. The more you ride your bike, the better you will be at controlling it.

Even if you can't ride off-road every day, you can practice these advanced skills around your neighborhood. Curbs are usually about the same height as logs, so you can practice hopping your bike up on them.

BALANCING

Balancing your bike while it's moving is easy. Balancing your bike when you aren't moving can be hard.

Talisyn, at right, shows how she stands on her pedals and keeps her weight evenly balanced. By quickly turning her handlebars right or left, she can balance.

Practice this move at very slow speeds. Soon you'll be able to stay in one place for as long as you need.

HOPPING

When jumping over a track or a log, you must hop. Jerad demonstrates this important—and flashy—skill.

Jerad rides at medium speed toward the log. Right before he gets to the log—as he stands on the pedals—he pulls up on the handlebars. This pulls his front wheel up and over the log. He leans forward and pulls up on his pedals by shifting his weight up and slightly forward. This motion lifts the back of the bike up and over the log. The back tire then rolls down the back of the obstacle.

Once you can do this move, you will use it many times on bike courses. You can also hop up on curbs.

CATCHING AIR

Riding over a bump fast enough to fly off of it is an exciting part of mountain biking. Control and balance are key when catching air.

Jason is moving fast down a trail. He approaches a bump in the path. He stands up on his pedals but stays low. Bending his arms, he rises over the bump. Jason stays centered over his pedals. As Jason rises, he pulls slightly on his handlebars to raise his front tire. He lands on his rear tire, which gives him better balance.

Jumping can be very dangerous. Before you catch air, make sure the landing area is free of obstacles. If you do fall, try to push your bike away from you because its sharp parts could injure you. Falling away from your bike isn't always possible, but that's one reason you always wear a helmet.

CARRY AND WALK

Sometimes nothing will get you up a hill. Other hills may be just too steep to go down. In these cases, you will want to carry or walk your bike up or down the hill.

On this page, Talisyn shows how to carry your bike. First, she dismounts while the bike is moving by swinging her right leg over the bike and jumping to the ground on both feet. She grabs the middle of the top bar and picks up the bike. Resting it on her shoulder, she holds onto the handlebars. At the top of the hill, Talisyn sets down her bike and mounts.

On this page, Nicole has decided to walk her bike instead of carrying it. After Nichole dismounts, she pushes the bike with her left hand on the seat and her right hand on the handlebars. When the terrain is very steep, she uses the bike for support.

OFF-ROAD TRAINING LOG

One good way to see your progress as a rider is to set up a riding schedule and keep a record of your rides.

If you plan to race, or if you just want to improve your endurance, consider a weekly schedule of rides. For instance, a schedule might look like this:

Monday: rest

Tuesday: fast ride with intervals of speed riding and hill climbing to build strength

Wednesday: slow ride to practice technical skills

Thursday: an hour or longer road ride

Friday: rest or a slow ride to recover

Saturday: long endurance ride for a few hours

Sunday: slow ride with friends

Set up your own training schedule after you've tried different things to see what works best for you. Then, during the week, keep a journal or log of your rides to see how you progress. You might include:

- Distance
- Time
- Heart rate
- Notes on skills you accomplished
- The weather
- How your bike performed
- Any repairs you needed
- What you saw
- Where you went
- How you felt during and after the ride

Your log will help you remember cool trails you found, how far you went that week, and maybe the animals you spotted on your mountain biking adventures.

HANDLING DITCHES

Ditches, small streams, and patches of eroded earth can cause problems for riders. Practice this move.

As Jake starts down into the ditch, he shifts his weight back. When he hits the bottom, he crouches lower for better traction. To climb the other side of the ditch, he shifts his weight off his front tire by bending his arms.

DIRT, ROCKS, AND SAND

Sometimes trails are just paths with room enough for one bike. These are called single track trails.

Packed dirt will give you the best traction, but rain or melting snow will leave dirt trails muddy for days. Don't ride on dirt trails too soon after it rains. Some mud is a fact of life in off-road riding, but riding on wet trails will damage them by speeding up erosion.

Small rocks or gravel may cause your tires to slip when you are pedaling hard uphill or going around corners. When you ride up a hill on loose gravel, keep your weight back on the bike. This will give you better traction on your rear tire so it won't spin out. Avoid turning on loose gravel. If you must turn on gravel, be ready to support yourself by dragging your foot on the side you are turning.

Big rocks can knock you off balance. It's a good idea to avoid them. Solid-rock areas give good traction, but they are rarely flat. Watch for your tires getting caught in crevices. Also, be careful not to catch your uphill pedal when it comes around at its lowest point.

Sand is often found at the bottom of hills. Sand can make controlling your bike difficult. Try riding straight ahead and pedaling constantly.

No two rides on a mountain bike will ever be the same. A familiar trail might change. A branch may have fallen, new rocks may be in your way, or rain may make it sloppy. Besides being a great form of exercise, mountain biking is fun. On a mountain bike, every ride is an adventure.

BIKE TALK

air pressure: A measurement of the amount of air in a tire.

balloon tires: Wide, flexible tires that provide a soft, cushioned ride.

beach-cruising bikes: One-speed bikes with large tires. Used for riding on sandy beaches.

brakes: Devices to stop or slow a bike by keeping the wheels from turning.

cranks: The pieces of metal that attach the pedals to the chainring.

derailleur: The mechanism that moves the chain from one sprocket to another. The front derailleur moves the chain on the chainwheel, and the rear derailleur moves the chain on the freewheel. The term is French, from "to take off the rail."

fat tires: Wide bike tires with deep treads.

feathering: Lightly squeezing and releasing the brakes in order to control the bike's speed.

fishtail: To swing out to one side and slide in an arc. The bike's back tire sometimes fishtails while a rider is braking, especially if the braking is done suddenly and vigorously.

frame: The basic metal structure of the bike.

gears: The system of controls used to make pedaling easier or harder by moving the chain from one set of sprockets to another.

hop: To raise a bike off the ground and over an obstacle.

momentum: The force of movement of an object in one direction.

saddle: The seat of the bike.

skidding: Scraping the tires on a surface by suddenly braking.

spin: To pedal rapidly to keep up speed.

spokes: Slender metal bars that support the rim of the wheel.

straightaway: A direct course, or part of a course, that doesn't turn.

toeclips: The cagelike pieces of equipment that hold a rider's feet to the pedals while riding.

traction: The friction that keeps bike tires from slipping on a surface.

wheel hubs: The metal parts that hold the spokes at the center of the wheels.

62

FURTHER READING

62

Gould, Tim, and Simon Burney. *Mountain Bike Racing*. San Francisco: Bicycle Books, 1992.

Hughes, Morgan. *Juli Furtado, Rugged Racer*. Minneapolis, MN: Lerner Publications, 1998.

Van der Plas, Robert. *Mountain Bike Book*. San Francisco: Bicycle Books, 1994.

Van der Plas, Robert. *Mountain Bike Magic*. San Francisco: Bicycle Books, 1991.

Woodward, Bob. *Sports Illustrated Mountain Biking: The Complete Guide*. New York: Sports Illustrated Winner's Circle Books, 1990.

FOR MORE INFORMATION

International Mountain Bike Association (IMBA)
P.O. Box 7578
Boulder, CO 80306
www.imba.com

National Off-Road Bicycle Association (NORBA)
c/o U.S.A. Cycling, Inc.
One Olympic Plaza
Colorado Springs, CO 80909
www.usacycling.org

Missy Giove is an exciting rider on the women's mountain bike circuit.

INDEX